D0596010

AMPLIFIED DOG

AMPLIFIED DOG

poems

CHARLES HARPER WEBB

RED HEN PRESS  LOS ANGELES

Amplified Dog

Copyright © 2006 by Charles Harper Webb

ALL RIGHTS RESERVED

No part of this book may be used or reproduced in any manner whatsoever without
the prior written permission of both the publisher and the copyright owner.

Book design by Michael Vukadinovich
Cover image "Charging Dog" by Renato Dornas (renato_dornas@yahoo.com.br)
Cover Design by Mark E. Cull

ISBN: 1-59709-022-0
Library of Congress Catalog Card Number: 2005929979

Published by Red Hen Press

The City of Los Angeles Cultural Affairs Department, California Arts Council, Los Angeles
County Arts Commission and National Endowment for the Arts partially support Red
Hen Press.

First Edition

ACKNOWLEDGEMENTS

The author would like to thank the editors of the following publications for first publishing these poems, sometimes in other versions:

5 AM: "Sperm Counts Are Falling," "Taming my Excesses"; American Poetry Review: "Bat Boy Joins Up"; Antioch Review: "Plato Didn't Feel Like a Great Philosopher"; Ascent: "Cyclops"; Atlanta Review and Best American Poetry, 2006: "Prayer to Tear the Sperm-Dam Down"; Chiron Review: "Surrender"; Cimarron Review: "Landscapes"; Cortland Review: "Reservations Confirmed"; Descant: "Cat Possessed by Poet Keats"; Free Lunch: "Librarian's Son"; Georgia Review: "Car Starting Late at Night," "Ooh My Soul"; Green Mountains Review: "Consider How the Toilet Overflows," "In Unromantic Times"; Kansas Quarterly: "Lost Bobbers," "The Animals Are Leaving"; Kestrel: "English," "King Solomon's Hit Man"; Laurel Review: "The End"; Michigan Quarterly Review: "My Wife Insists that, on our First Date, I Told Her I Had Seven Kinds of Hair," "The New World Book of Webbs," "Two Heroes"; Mid-American Review: "Does Time Really Exist?"; Painted Bride Quarterly: "Us and Them"; Paris Review: "Erik Discovers, Among Other Things, His Hands"; Pearl: "Sad Bus"; Ploughshares: "I Never Had an Imaginary Friend," "Pumpkin Envy," "Taking Out Trash"; Poet Lore: "Scuba Heaven"; Poetry International: "Daddy's Disease," "How to Live," "Tear-Stained Confetti"; Prairie Schooner: "In the Beginning Was the Word," "My Son Is Called 'Developmentally Delayed'"; Rattle: "Heat Wave"; RiversEdge: "Kissing"; Tampa Review: "A Grand Opening of Hearts," "Seducing Sleep"; Tar River Poetry: "Amateurs"; The Panhandler: "Mysteries"; Third Coast: "Amplified Dog"; TriQuarterly: "How I Know I'm Not a Spiritual Master"; Virginia Quarterly Review: "A Meal Not Eaten," "Hummingbirds," "The Open-Air Recital Survived a Shaky Start"; Washington Square: "Post-Modern Life"; West Branch: "Brain Damage," "I Never Promised You a Worm Farm" "The Animals Are Leaving" appeared in Poetry from A to Z; Bradbury Press (MacMillan Publishing Company), 1994. "Kissing" appeared in Touched By Eros, Live Poets Society, 2002. "Reservations Confirmed" appeared in Air Fare, Sarabande Books, 2004. "Cat Possessed by Poet Keats" won the Betsy Colquitt Poetry Award for the best poem published in 2002 by Descant magazine. "The Open-Air Recital Survived A Shaky Start" and "A Meal Not Eaten" won the Emily Clark Balch Prize for the best poems published in 2003 by Virginia Quarterly Review.

I am grateful to the Mrs. Giles Whiting Foundation and the John Simon Guggenheim Foundation for fellowships that supported the writing of many of these poems.

The writing of this book was partially funded by California State University, Long Beach, Scholarly and Creative Activities Awards.

Special thanks to Ron Koertge, Richard Garcia, Judith Taylor, and Aliki Barnstone for invaluable editorial assistance, and to Edward Hirsch, who got the train on track.

for Karen and Erik

CONTENTS

AMPLIFIED DOG

AMPLIFIED DOG

"What's that?!" whispers my wife.
Through thick layers of sleep, I hear a voice
outside. Distorted. Blaring.

I shuffle to the window. Full moon gleams
on the blue plastic I spread to funnel off
El Niño rains. The night stays still. My feet

leak heat, so I'm moving back to bed
when the voice starts to sing. In Spanish.
Amplified—by what? A blown-out stereo?

"Should we call the cops?" whispers my wife.
"No. It's nothing," I say. Then the dog
speaks: Woof!—distorted as the song.

A scene tunes in: A man is swigging Cuervo Gold.
His wife, Dalila's, gone. His heart hurts,
so he pulls out the sound system he's kept

since he sang in Los Pochos, back when he met her.
Maybe she'll hear him from Ramon's,
four blocks away. Maybe she'll throw on

her clothes while Ramon, belly swaying
in pink boxers, can't hold her back . . .
No. So the man lets Paco in.

Tail-wagging Paco: man's best friend.
"She loved you more than me," he says,
and sets the mike to Paco's height. "Call her, boy."

Paco sniffs the mike, then barks, and hears
his voice—Woof!—louder than it's ever been.
How many times has he stood in the yard straining

to warn people how much they're messing up?
Woof! Woof! all day. But they won't hear.
They never learn. Hector, as usual, passes out.

Hector—his friend, who couldn't smell trouble
when Dalila reeked of it. Poor Hector, stupid and sad,
just like a man. So Paco calls his warning

as the moon tunnels through black night to silver sky.
Woof! *The world you've made stinks to high heaven.*
Woof! *You're mean to one another.* Woof!

You let bad people lead you. Woof! *You work too much,
and don't enjoy enough. You waste your time
on trivialities.* Woof! *Even sex is work for you.*

Paco loves the way his voice rattles the house,
then flies off in all directions
like pigeons when he runs right into them.

"If it's nothing," my wife says, "come back to bed."
"Quiet," I growl under my breath. "Paco,
I'm here. I'm listening."

I

OOH MY SOUL
     —Little Richard

By night, ghosts roam Aunt Ermyn's
elm-shrouded, hundred-year-old home.
By day, my cousin Pete, just out of high school
combs his duck-tail and keeps time
to records with his creaky rocking chair.
I'm in the hall, creating all-star teams
of baseball cards when, blaring
through Pete's open door, I hear . . .
war-drums? Or is it a runaway train?
Keepa knockin' but you cain't come in,
some kind of preacher shrieks,
then squeals like tires around a curve.
Those chugging drums, smoking piano,
squawking duck-call saxophones
make me feel like an oil rig ready to blow.
I see wells pumping, teeter-totters bumping,
giant turtle-heads working out and in
as bronco riders wave tall hats in the air.
I see girls twirling, dresses swirling
high over their underwear,
guys doing splits, or inch-worming
across the floor.
                    It makes me want
to slam my head back and forth
like a paddle ball—to jump, shout, bang
my hands on walls, and flap them
in the air—to fall onto the ground
and writhe, flail, roar like Johnny Cerna
in his famous Kiddieland tantrum.
Keepa knockin' but you cain't come in,
the preacher howls. But I *am* in.
I'm in the living room, Bandstand on TV,
Dad ranting, "Goddamn Congo Beat!"
I'm in the back seat of his Ford
a decade later, learning what that beat
could be. I'm in my first band, hoarse

from screaming "Long Tall Sally."
I'm in my college dorm, trying to jam
that wild abandon into poems.
I'm in my car, heading for work
when *Good Golly, Miss Molly!*
catapults out of my Blaupunkt stereo.
I'm walking into Pete's bedroom,
where I've never dared to go. Oh,
womp bompalumomp, a lomp bam boom!
I'm not thinking in words, but I know
I've spent my seven years rehearsing
how to feel this way. It's more exciting
than a touchdown any day, or a home run,
a gunfight, hurricane waves at Galveston,
a five-pound bass on a cane pole.
"What is that?" I ask Pete. He says,
"Rock and roll."

I NEVER HAD AN IMAGINARY FRIEND

I would've called him Ice Cream, or Monopoly,
or Grand Slam: something I especially liked.
He'd have played catch with me when no one else

was home. He could have come from planet Fazbag,
where God taught him kung fu. He might
have traded crescent kicks with Christ. Or been a girl.

Maybe on Fazbag, boys and girls weren't shoved
apart by the snarling referee Propriety,
when all they wanted was to clinch. My friend

might not have been human. He might have had
five heads, or wings and scales, or tentacles.
She might have been a brain floating in a jar,

a pulsing blob, or a rock who saw the future
and, by thumping, told me what to do.
Maybe I did have such a friend before adulthood's

German housemaid scrubbed the memory away.
Everything seemed friendly in those days:
the grass that left green blessings on my pants,

the baseball glove that couldn't wait to hold my hand,
even the sun which, when I went shirtless at the beach,
stared at me with so much love I burned.

MY WIFE INSISTS THAT, ON OUR FIRST DATE, I TOLD HER
I HAD SEVEN KINDS OF HAIR

Straight, frizzy, chest, nose, pubic . . . what was I thinking?
Seven is special, I know. Seven thieves. Seven
wonders, sleepers, worthies, gables, cities, seventh

sons of seventh sons with more mojo than seven men.
We ate at Mogo's, I remember, where we chose
from a dozen kinds of vegetables, as well as chicken,

turkey, pork, and beef. The chef spilled our choices
onto a grill, then moved from pile to sizzling pile,
chopped, smoothed, arranged until, with his skilled

spatula, he heaped hot meals into the begging bowls
we both thrust out. I led us to a dim corner,
well aware that of the three body types, six kinds

of laughs, five kinds of breasts, and eight varieties
of lips, hers held the summit of each heap. Her long,
dark hair and sapphire eyes made my hands shake.

Her shape unhinged my diaphragm. I'll bet I groped
in my suddenly dim brain, and spilled whatever
I found onto our talk, I was so eager to keep it sizzling,

so hungry to seem a man whose invention never failed,
well-endowed with all good things, including hair.
"At least one kind," I must have meant, "is right for you."

THE NEW WORLD BOOK OF WEBBS

"I have exciting news for you and all Webbs."
—Miles. S. Webb

The brochure shows a boat passing the Statue of Liberty
while its cargo of immigrants stand gaping,
and one small boy—dressed better than the rest—
watches from a director's chair. He,
obviously, is the Webb. Simple but aristocratic.
Poor, but destined for greatness. Set apart

from the Smiths and Joneses, the Rothblatts
and Steins, the Schmidts and Hampys, the Mancusos
and Malvinos and Mendozas and Tatsuis
and Chus, by "the distinguished Webb name."
Excitement steams from Miles S. Webb's letter to me.
The very type leaps up and down. Just buy

his book, and I will learn (I'm guessing)
about Thomas Webb, famous for his kippered
herring jokes, and Dan Webb of the talking armpits,
and Genevieve Webb, convinced her left
and right feet were reversed. I'll learn the inside story
of Solomon Webb, Dover's greatest circus geek,

and Lady Messalina Webb, transported to Australia
with her husband, Sir Caleb Webb,
son of the merkin-maker Jemmie Webb of Kent.
Best of all, inside the bonus *Webb International Directory*,
one among 104,352 Webb households in the world,
there I'll be: the very Webb who woke this morning

at 5:53 when his new sprinklers ratcheted on
with the screech of strangled grebes—the Webb
who lolled in bed, loving the artificial rain, then cracked
his drapes and saw fat drops annoint his porch,
and a hummingbird light on a hair-thin twig,
then buzz away when the sprinklers hissed off.

The lawn lay drinking, then—each blade
with its own history, each listed in the Book of Heaven
(Grandma Webb from Yorkshire used to say),
each destined to be cut later this morning by José,
one of 98,998 people to bear (his letter states)
the "brave and glory-dripping name Cortez."

CAT POSSESSED BY POET KEATS

Cockney John could have sneaked in while Mr.
Meepers lay unconscious with an abscess
At the vet's. Or did the surgeon-poet
Squeak in later, through the draining tube
Stuck in the poor cat's head? It's certain

That—stretched in my lap, my hands conducting
The concerto of his purr—he said,
No, no, go not to Lethe, neither twist
Wolf's bane, tight-rooted, for its poisonous wine.
Within a week, he'd rattled off "Endymion,"

"The Eve of Saint Agnes," "La Belle
Dame Sans Merci," plus all the odes.
He liked to sit with Kate and me, watching
Clouds dirigible across the sky,
The sun's last rays igniting them

As mockingbirds extemporized. Kate recognized
The most melodious pair: Felix and Fanny
Mendelssohn. Toadily, Kate's Southwest
Toad, turned out to be Georgia O'Keefe;
Nigel the Hedgehog was Shakespeare;

Tchaikovsky, Yeats, Bach, and Vermeer flocked
To my back yard, chattering. Even
The caravans of ants proved to be artists,
Though minor ones, like me. First
Among us all was Keats, making us laugh

With his "Mra-*raa*!" and "Tee Wang Dillo Dee,"
The "amen to nonsense" which he used
If I got pretentious, fought with Kate
Over trivialities, or didn't pay
Attention as he caught flies, chased pink

Ribbons, wrestled his jingling mouse.
It was Keats, I know, who called the others
To my house, and convinced Kate to marry me—
Kate, whose love offsets my lack of genius,
And makes me capable of anything.

SPERM COUNTS ARE FALLING

Guys today aren't half the men our fathers were,
Scientists say. Though we're taller, faster, stronger,
And weigh more. Though we've had more
Lovers, and done more with them. Sperm counts are falling—

Down by half in fifty years.
Though we have lap-top computers, spread sheets, frequent flyer
    miles—
Though we have jobs where we're paid to sit and think,
Sperm counts are falling.

I don't want this to be true.
I don't want to be like those Florida 'gators turned by pesticides
    into virtual girls.
I don't want wombs replaced by Pyrex tubes.
All the same, sperm counts are falling. Look at me—

In better shape than kids a third my age,
My life-expectancy Bungeed out past eighty years.
I kick-box four times a week, lift weights, hunt, fish and don't
    take guff;
That doesn't keep sperm counts from falling.

Are feminists to blame? Researchers say
That when male monkeys lose status, their sperm counts fall.
But a running back more celebrated than Christmas can't get
    (the *Star* relates) his giant penis up.
A guitar hero comes too soon;

A movie idol likes one woman with two boys;
Another one prefers gerbils.
Should we fault the Ozone Hole?
Sperm counts are falling as housing prices soar.

GNPs skyrocket while third-world babies die.
Is God aborting Mission: Multiply?
Gangsters still gain points by leaving trails of kids.
I got a girl pregnant before I could vote. (Thanks, Supreme Court,
    for Roe v Wade.)

But I'm less horny nowadays. Is that just age?
I don't laugh at sexist jokes.
I read women's eyes before I hold their doors.
I understand all parts of "No." Is it because sperm counts are falling

That fights get more lethal week by week?
A "good butt-kicking" used to mean a shiner and a bloody nose.
Now a speed freak ice-picks your eyes, castrates, and pre-guts you
    for the morgue.
Now a ten-year-old shoots you twenty times, rapes your toddler,
    and pimps her on the street.

I feel my sperm count falling as I drive through LA, or go to work,
    or out to eat.
Though I have a tough-guy goatee, hairy chest, and never cry,
Sperm counts are falling.
My wife and I may want a child.

PUMPKIN-ENVY

How many hours did I lie in bed, thought stapling
my sixteen-year-old arms to the sheets,
thought's curare, when I finally did dial Tami Jamison,
numbing my lips too much to speak?

How often did I think, "I'm dead," feeling
my strength leak away, phlegm drown my lungs,
sarcomas thrust like red toads up out of my skin
in the three days between the blood-drawing

and the doctor's benediction: "Negative."
Thought is a rope that pulls the kite out of the sky—
a cramp that locks the boxer's chin as fists hiss
toward his head. "What sharks?" my friend demands,

launching the sea-kayak that gives him so much fun.
How many odes would Keats have traded for one
night with Fanny Brawne? What did understanding do
for Nietzsche, but make him more insane?

Thought is more deadly than crack or heroin.
Its pipe to my lips, its needle in my vein,
I loll in my dark room, and envy pumpkin vines.
Whatever's in their way, they overrun. Unafraid

of blight, birds, drought, or humans' being,
they stretch out in the heat, let their roots drink deep
and—never giving a thought to anything—
make a million copies of the sun.

I NEVER PROMISED YOU A WORM FARM

When her psychology patients start her wishing
for a padded cell, Kate digs up her Earthworm Fantasy:
barrels of loam in our basement, crawling with worms;
the kitchen crowded with milk-cartons incubating worms;
"Webb's Worm Farm" in vermiform letters on our door.

She'd sell to fishermen at first, then worm her way
into health food. (Organic worm-meal: pure protein.)
A Super Bowl blitz, with praise from Budweiser's chameleons
would break her into grocery stores, then restaurants—
worm Wellington, worm teriyaki, mu shu worms.

She was raising *mealworms* when we met: beetle-larvae,
that mostly went to feed her Southwest toads.
A few matured, though, scaled their Tupperware bowl,
and burrowed in her bed, with me inside.
"I have a gift for growing worms," she likes to say.

So when she reads how a Canadian biologist
developed foot-long fluorescent orange, purple,
red, or green night-crawlers that smell like garlic
or anything they eat, she starts clearing the basement.
That's when—feeling like the kind of spoilsport

who'd tell a young DaVinci to stop doodling and deliver
the damn pizzas—I say no; it's not practical,
not esthetic, not happening while I live here.
She smiles and says, "I was just kidding."
Was she? Really? No matter how deeply we love,

how thoroughly we think we know someone,
who ever sees the basement of another mind?
Who knows what grows, fluorescent and wriggling,
smelling of garlic or road-kill or April roses,
way down there?

KISSING

"Why is that fun?" I wondered as a kid—
the press of mouths, rubbing of lips,
sharing of saliva and stinks: peanut butter
with jack cheese, tuna with milk.

Did the kissers mean to form an air-tight seal?
Would they twist together like lead pipes?
Were their skulls like tortoises trying to mate?
Later, I learned that some kissers are vacuums,

eager to yank out their partner's guts.
Some are shuttles that link up, hoping
to construct a safe station in space.
Some lips, when kissed, are rubber bumpers;

others, suction cups. In the "French kiss,"
tongues embrace like slippery snakes.
Kissing, for men, is more intimate than sex;
the mouth's portcullis lifts to let the female in.

If breath is life, and human life has soul,
a kiss is two souls mingling. But breath is waste,
a by-product of oxidation; so shared breath
is shared excreta—intimate, yes; but romantic?

Not all cultures kiss. Some tribes rub noses,
or just fuck, struggling not to knock heads.
Kissing may be a safety precaution for heads,
like bracing melons so they won't roll off a truck.

I've felt lessened by kissing—emotionally shrunk.
With you, though, it's a perfect trade.
We part, having given what we have in surplus,
having gained exactly what we need.

PRAYER TO TEAR THE SPERM-DAM DOWN

> *Because we need to remember / that memory will end, let the*
> *womb remain / untouched.*
> *—from "Prayer to Seal up the Wombdoor" by Suzanne Paola*

Because we know our lives will end,
Let the vagina host a huge party, and let the penis come.

Let it come nude, without a raincoat.
Let it come rich, and leave with coffers drained.

Throw the prostate's flood-gates open.
Let sperm crowd the womb full as a World Cup stadium.

Let them flip and wriggle like a mackerel shoal.
Let babies leap into being like atoms after the Big Bang.

Let's celebrate fullness, roundness, gravidity.
Let's worship generation—this one,

And the next, and next, forever.
Let's adore the progression: protozoan to guppy

To salamander to slow loris to Shakespeare.
Forget Caligula. Forget Hitler. Mistakes

Were made. Let's celebrate our own faces
Grinning back at us across ten thousand years.

Let's get this straight: Earth doesn't care if it's overrun—
if it's green or brown or black, rain forest, desert, or ice pack.

A paper mill is sweet as lavender to Earth,
Which has no sense of smell, and doesn't care

If roads gouge it, or industries fume into its air.
Beetles don't care. Or crows,

Or whales, despite their singing and big brains.
Sure, rabbits feel. Spicebush swallowtails

Feel their proboscides slide into flowers'
Honey-pots, which may feel too,

But lack the brains to care. Even if beagles
Are mournful as they look—

Even if great apes grieve, wage war, catch termites
With twigs, and say in sign language,

"Ca-ca on your head," they still don't care.
Or if they do—well, join the club.

We humans care so much, some of us dub life
A *vale of tears*, and see heaven as oblivion.

Some pray, for Earth's sake, not to be reborn.
Wake up! Earth will be charred by the exploding sun,

Blasted to dust, reduced to quarks, and still not care.
If some people enjoy their lives too much

To share, let them not share. If some despise themselves
Too much to reproduce, let them disappear.

If some perceive themselves as a disease, let them
Take the cure, and go extinct. It's immaterial to Earth.

Let people realize this, or not. Earth doesn't care.
I do, and celebrate my own fecundity.

I celebrate my wife's ovaries, her fallopian tubes
Down which, like monthly paychecks,

Gold eggs roll. I celebrate the body's changing.
(Might as well; it changes anyway.)

I celebrate gestation, water breaking,
The dash to the hospital, the staff descending,

Malpractice policies in hand. I celebrate
Dilation of the cervix, doctors in green scrubs,

And even (since I won't get one) the episiotomy.
I'll celebrate my bloody, dripping son, head deformed

By thrusting against the world's door.
Let it open wide for him. Let others make room for him.

Let his imagination shine like God's.
Let his caring change the face of everything.

CYCLOPS

More monstrous than Scylla, since more human—
more hideous than the Sirens, who were beautiful
sometimes—Polyphemus hunkered in his cave,

lifting warriors, as they shrieked and shit themselves,
toward the slavering mouth below his one huge eye.
The horror of him bounding over rocks

in *Sinbad's Seven Voyages* still wakes me
after forty years. Now doctors know
that, if they disrupt one gene, an embryonic tadpole's

eyes don't separate, but become a single
deep ocular pool. The same thing happens
with birds, leaving no doubt that it could

happen in humans, and by Murphy's Law, *has*
happened, and sometimes the monster lived.
How could the Mycenaean mother explain

the nightmare wailing in her hands, except to say
Poseidon raped her as she bathed?
What could be done but leave the sacred

offspring on a rocky island to herd sheep
and scour the rocks for shipwrecked men?
No wonder Odysseus was praised for killing him.

No wonder, after his death, Polyphemus grew in myth
from a gnarled four-foot-ten, to taller than a pine.
No wonder yogis feel a third eye where their two

began, and healthy brain cells quail to think
of Polyphemus where he waits within:
Blinded. Roaring.

MY SON IS CALLED "DEVELOPMENTALLY DELAYED"

Is it so bad if he drops Doctor's stuffed frog? Maybe
it stinks of alien drool. Maybe his head wobbles
because it's packed with brains! Once again I'm at the mercy

of "experts" like Coach Blummer, who halved my batting
average, adjusting my swing—like the Einstein
who changed my clutch when my fuel pump was clogged—

like those old fools who called the shots in Vietnam.
Will hospitals bleed me dry? Will my wife and I
shun each other like partners in a shameful crime?

When friends ask, "How's your son?" what should I say?
I don't see high spirits when his arms and legs
flail now; I see pathology. When I hear the bleats

and squawks we've called "talking," I wonder if he'll ever
say "Da Da," let alone "I do." "Babies develop differently.
Don't worry yet," the doctor says. Thanks hugely,

Doc—you've fired up the Self-Fulfilling Prophecy,
then jumped out of the cab. All I can do as it rolls
toward me, is kiss my wife goodnight, and flee into Sleep.

(I dream I'm at my army physical. We drop our pants.
The doctor weeps, "This man has *subsequent vagina!*")
When I wake, red-eyed, all I can do is hope

that what's stuck in my son breaks free, and he leaps
forward, passing milestones in a blur. Little guy
gurgling in your crib—all I can do is pray to the Big Void

that, years from now, you'll read this in a glance,
then roll your strong arm around my shoulder.
"Dad, you always were a little slow," you'll say.

CONSIDER HOW THE TOILET OVERFLOWS,

water pouring over porcelain
white as a wentletrap.
It could be a Roman fountain,
or a spring gurgling

out of a chalk mountain
to sustain a town. Think
how you pump the plunger,
and brown sludge—

rich, fecund as the Nile—
floods the shower stall.
Think how the plumber
drives up, baseball cap

bleached pale as ivory,
overalls spotted
as a robin's egg.
Think of the "snake"

he directs, head fluted
as a spear-tip, body
coiled in an orange shell.
Think how that lithe

snake-length feels
into the unknown.
Picture the pipes
where microbes row

translucent oars,
and twirl like dust
in streams of sun.
Think of the body's waste

transformed, its recycling
begun. Think
of the obstruction found,
the drain's vortex

spinning like a ballerina
as the plumber grins
and the owner's fear *glug-
glugs* away. Think of the snake

pulled out, a sopping rag
snagged on its tongue.
Think of that rag flushed
by some child of former owners,

some exhausted maid.
Think of it hiding
in the pipes, absorbing
blackness from its tunnel-home.

Think of it waving, limber
as a water plant—
slipping through pipes
like a browsing fish—

exploring like a submarine
until, bunched up
by the power of hydraulics,
it tells the water, "Stop!"

Think of that Nautilus
drawn back into sunlight:
dripping secrets scented
with the dark and deep.

PLATO DIDN'T FEEL LIKE A GREAT PHILOSOPHER

when, late for a wedding, he threw on his best white *chiton*,
and his wife snickered at the yellow stains.
He wished, then, he'd never heard of Socrates,
and had pursued wine-selling, vase-making, medicine—
something that coupled cachet with serious cash.

Students fled his Academy to drink at Dionysios's place,
or to gamble with Zeno, who always bet no one
would cross the finish line. They loved to fool around
with maenads, then show off infected hickies.
A few dunces even dropped out to write poems.

In Plato's ideal world, students hungered for Truth.
He was a Hero there: muscled like a god,
beautiful girls and boys fighting to sleep with him,
their Philosopher-King, renowned
for fairness and good sense. No way in hades

was he the pot-bellied butt of dirty dithyrambs.
No student won fame splatting spitwads
onto his bald head. In that perfect world, he never woke
at night as I do after a fight with Kate,
and can't remember who I am or what I've done.

TEAR-STAINED CONFETTI

If my son wants his bottle, he cries.
If his diaper needs changing, he cries.
If he's too cold or hot, if light glares in his eyes,

if a horn blares outside and startles him, he cries.
If he flails his arms and bops his nose, he cries.
He'll tantrum pretty soon. But I?—

the alarm clock blasts me out of bed; cold bores
into my skin; my ankle, which I turned
on the treadmill, spikes pain to my forehead;

I cut myself shaving, and recall I have to meet at 9:00
a student whose term paper was repossessed
with his car, and who calls this "an act of God."

Five minutes awake, I could have cried a dozen times.
But adulthood means squelching more than tears.
Consider truth—"the artist's stock-in-trade," I hear.

Ha! If artists told the truth each time they chiseled
a finger, or life swindled them, the David
would be a pile of scree; Dali's "Soft Construction

with Boiled Beans" would be a heap
of kindling and paint-splashed canvas shreds
no different from Watteau's bucolic dreams.

This very book would be tear-stained confetti
if I didn't straitjacket my nerves,
and scratch these words in my hurried

hand before I sprint (stubbing my toe
on a toy truck) to my boy's crib, where I rearrange
the blanket he's kicked off his cold legs,

pick him up, give him his bottle (warmed),
and soothe him with that classic human lie:
"Ssh. Everything's all right."

THE ANIMALS ARE LEAVING

One by one, like guests at a late party,
They shake our hands and step into the dark:
Arabian ostrich; Long-eared kit fox; Mysterious starling.

One by one, like sheep counted to close our eyes,
They leap the fence and disappear into the woods:
Atlas bear; Passenger pigeon; North Island laughing owl;
Great auk; Dodo; Eastern wapiti; Badlands bighorn sheep.

One by one, like grade school friends,
They move away and fade out of our memory:
Portuguese ibex; Blue buck; Auroch; Oregon bison;
Spanish imperial eagle; Japanese wolf; Hawksbill
Sea turtle; Cape lion; Heath hen; Raiatea thrush.

One by one, like children at a fire drill, they march outside,
And keep marching, though teachers cry, "Come back!"
Waved albatross; White-bearded spider monkey;
Pygmy chimpanzee; Australian night parrot;
Turquoise parakeet; Indian cheetah; Korean tiger;
Eastern harbor seal; Ceylon elephant; Great Indian rhinoceros.

One by one, like actors after a play that ran for years
And wowed the world, they link their hands and bow
Before the curtain falls.

II

HOW YOU KNOW YOU'RE NOT A SPIRITUAL MASTER

"All suffering comes from attachment."
—The Buddha

You'd give anything to be photographed for *People*
in a muscle shirt (with muscles) on a vintage Harley
on a Grecian beach during the filming of *Captain Correlli's
Mandolin*, costarring Penelope Cruz and Christian Bale.
You'd kill to be Enrique, son of Julio Iglesias, proud

that your "way with women" "provokes whispers"
as you "squire" *American Pie* beauty Shannon Elizabeth
to your twenty-fifth birthday party at Le Colonial,
despite her being engaged to another man.
If only you could sit for hours pondering the Absolute

(not the vodka)! You have more attachments
than a dentistry machine; therefore, you suffer.
Criticized by your wife, you can't assume
the lotus posture while cosmic resonance rolls up
from your deepest chakras, and your astral body drifts

among the stars. You stare at "Gorgeous George"
Clooney in his "impeccable" tux escorting Uma Thurman
in her "practically nonexistent Gaultier ensemble"
(lace, mirrors, and silver lamé) which she "ditched
in favor of a blue Ferretti number" to wind up

her Cannes afternoon, and you think, "I'd die to have
his life, or for that matter, hers." You wouldn't feel that way
if you were a Bodhisattva, smoothing compassion's
aloe across the sunburned earth—if you could quip
to fellow crucifixees, "Dudes, hang loose"—

if you ever, for a moment, could live in that moment
instead of ricocheting between a past
in which you weren't, and a future in which you'll never be
Quentin Tarrantino "clowning with Juliette Lewis"
at a Hollywood Premiere, or John Travolta "mugging

with buddy Sly Stallone" outside Mann's Theatre,
or even Zadie Smith: daughter of a London ad executive
and a Jamaican model-turned-child-psychoanalyst.
This young author of *White Teeth* "bites into life
as a literary star," looking ultra-bright, tough, beautiful,

and bored. She calls "the fame game" "tiresome,"
and almost certainly returns from her photo shoot
to some Zen cell where, meditating on the letter B
in *Big Deal,* she'll close her "sultry brown eyes,"
and breathing from her diaphragm, (continue to) rise.

DADDY'S DISEASE

I have to pull off the freeway when, on my Recorded Book,
      the atheist Bazarov's parents kneel beside his bed,
           weeping and praying while he dies of fever.

At lunch, reading "Farewell, thou child
      of my right hand, and joy," I bang shut the anthology
           to keep from blubbering on my California rolls.

I—lover of the caustic phrase and dry ice sneer—
      can't bear to see my son's outgrown overalls.
           In his crib, he hides his head, then squealing,

shoves the sheet away. For him, it's child's play
      to pop in and out of this world;
           but I drag around the cast iron truth all day.

IN UNROMANTIC TIMES

No wind swirls around this house, making
The banshee-windows whine, shaking the door
Like Frankenstein's wretch trying to break in.
Street lamps illuminate no sad-eyed-girl-
From-a-good-family, who, having trudged

Miles in a downpour to bear her son
(Destined for greatness), dies among strangers.
Our highwaymen do not wear French cocked hats,
Or lace collars, or coats of claret velvet,
Or boots up to the thigh over cinnamon

Breeches of doe-skin. Young gentlemen
Don't sweep through fifty-room chateaus-
With-colonnades, their red silk capes flapping behind.
They do not press one hand (palm out)
To their foreheads. In their studies, at rosewood

Desks inlaid with mother-of-pearl,
They do not weep over Hector's speech
To Andromache. They do not write,
With quill pens, sonnets to their cruel beloved,
Or sip sorrow like plum wine snatched

From corsairs on the China Sea. They don't
Give up titles and lands, then, slammed by rain
Hard as grapeshot, dash off to die
In some noble foreign war. There is no war
Worth dying for, no glorious pain.

TWO HEROES

Like me mounting that mechanical bull, Dolon
must have thought "Uh-oh," as he shot off
into the night. "Ill-favored but fast," he should
have been snoring beside his slow, ill-favored wife.
But when Hector, monstrous by torchlight,

offered a chariot and two stallions as reward
for spying on the Greeks, Dolon pictured himself
cantering through Troy while girls who'd swooned
for pretty-boy Paris flopped down for him,
and men who'd ridiculed him knew how wrong

they'd been. "My pride as a man urges me to go,"
he blurted, pulling on The Iliad's only
"weasel hat." Minutes later, two Greeks
spied him: Diomedes of the Great War Cry,
and Odysseus, who'd have his own epic someday.

These were the kind of men Dolon loathed most,
and idolized: strutting and flexing in bronze gear,
eager to lop off this man's arm, spear that man's groin,
cleave another's face "so that his eyes popped out
and his brain plopped in pieces on the ground."

Ordered to box Benny Mongonia in P.E.,
like Dolon, I ran. In all The Iliad, he is the only man
described as "like a doe that flees bleating before hounds."
When Diomedes hurled a spear over his head,
Dolon froze, "teeth chattering, pale with fear."

When the Greeks sauntered up, he "burst into tears,"
as I did (almost) when Donnie Johns and Ray Montez
asked me who ratted on their cheating ring.
Other captives offered ransom: bronze and gold.
Only Dolon squealed like me. Caught stealing baseball cards,

I begged to "wear a wire" and finger friends—anything
if the crew-cut guard would let me go, please, *please*.
Dolon mapped out the whole Trojan line, helpfully
highlighting where to find the King of Thrace,
whose jeweled chariot had made him gag on jealousy.

Despite my blubbering, the guard called my dad.
As for Dolon—when he'd spilled his beans, filled
his underwear, and was begging mercy
on his knees, Diomedes sliced off his ill-favored head,
"still shrieking when his mouth bit the sand."

SURRENDER

I give up righteous indignation: my clenched teeth
and knotted fists. I leap off adrenaline's runaway train.
I give my flak suit to Good Will, and throw in the bloody towel.

When an acromegalic berates me for preferring "pretty girls,"
I ask her out, I spend big bucks on her, I swear to change
my life. I want to join the bruise-kneed ranks of the good

losers. (Insurance men—dump your worst policies on me!)
I want to smile at the DMV clerk through his haze
of after-shave as he insists there is no record of my car.

That explains why I get nowhere. To hell
with exercise, the decades' bench press straining to crush me.
I welcome old age like a friend I picked a fight with,

and have missed ever since. I give up battling gardeners;
I want my trees to look like arrows, fletched only at the top:
five hundred times quintuple amputees.

Pay the blind surgeon, and get him out of here.
Let mufflers of flab collect under my chin; let arthritis
wrap me in its aching rags. I want to come in last, bring up

the rear, eat after everyone is served, limp to the end
of the line, and like it there. Saints, hermits, suicides were right!
I want to cash out my accounts and equities, then shove

the sum at the first bum who brandishes a misspelled sign,
calls me a jive chump, and thrusts a crusty paw at me.
Let him lug the cement briefcases of solvency until his elbows

stretch down past his knees. Hand him my Good Citizen's
Electric Boxers with Bonus Self-Recharging Batteries,
and let him have a big surprise.

RESERVATIONS CONFIRMED

The ticket settles on my desk: a paper tongue
pronouncing "Go away"; a flattened seed
from which a thousand-mile leap through the air can grow.

It's pure potential: a vacation-to-be
the way an apple is a pie-to-be,
a bullet is a death-to-be. Or is the future

pressed into it inalterably—woven between
the slicked fibers like secret threads
from the U.S. Treasury? Is my flight number

already flashing as cameras grind and the newly-
bereaved moan? Or does it gleam under Arrivals,
digits turned innocuous as those that didn't

win the raffle for a new Ford truck?
If, somewhere, I'm en route right now, am I
praying the winged ballpoint I'm strapped into

will write on Denver's runway, "Safe and Sound"?
Was my pocket picked in Burbank,
and I've just noticed at thirty thousand feet?

Am I smiling as the clouds' icefields melt
to smoky wisps, revealing lakes below
like Chinese dragons embroidered in blue?

Lifting my ticket, do I hold a *bon voyage*,
or boiling jet streams, roaring thunderstorms,
the plane bounced like a boat on cast iron seas,

then the lightning flash, the dizzy plunge,
perfectly aware (amid the shrieks and prayers)
that, live or die, I won't survive the fall?

SAD BUS

Its doors hiss open, and weeping pours out—
From the driver with his gray beard and cup-handle ears—
From the tall guy whose legs jut into the aisle, whose copper skin
    and eagle-beak make him look Sioux, mourning his tribe—

From the gangbanger in plaid who, even as he whimpers, thrusts his
    leg against a young chicana, who finds this more reason to cry—
From the redhead who wore her workout leotard to show her shape,
    which is nothing to cry about—
From the parents who shush their baby's screams while their own tears
    drench his Lion King peejays.

The whole bus shudders and shakes.
The windshield-wipers can't keep tears from its glass eyes.
Does the driver despise his job?

Have all his riders quarreled with spouses too, and don't see how their
    marriage can survive?
Do their nagging pains bode future agony?
Have both their parents died, and now the world seems gray and alien
    as Martian stone?

I sniffle as my fare drops down the steel, trap-bottomed hole.
I stagger to an empty seat, and wail.
In my own house, I don't feel this much at home.

LOST BOBBERS

Where do they go, those blinking plastic eyes
that scan for fish; those red-and-white basketballs
that bluegills dribble around lily pads;
those cork cigars that tilt and fall
over like drunks; those bubbles clear as foam
riding the current's rush?
                              When I was nine,
I found nine good ones sloshing in a hollow log,
filled my tackle box and ran home, feeling rich.
Every day, kids find a few nested on shore,
or circling in pools, tired fish still on the line.
The rest escape.
                      Do they keep drifting
to the sea, then roam like Flying Dutchmen
until Judgement Day? Do they crack on rocks
and sink, flickering down to lie with gold
doubloons and sailors' bones?
                                  I want them
to float on and on, past the horizon,
off the world's edge to a place where all children
who've ever lived—even those their parents
hated, those beaten and worked to death,
tortured and starved—stand side-by-side on one
long pier, each with a fishing rod stretched
over the green water's fall and rise.
                                    Hearts bouncing,
they watch the bobbers bump and glide
against the tide until one dives,
and a child feels the fish, potent as blood,
the pulsing power of its otherness.
"Daddy! Help!" the child screams.
And Daddy comes running. "Reel! Reel!
That's the way," he yells, and grasps the rod
just enough to ease the strain, not enough
to steal the glory as the sky ignites
and night drags the sun's gold bobber down.

ERIK DISCOVERS, AMONG OTHER THINGS,
HIS HANDS

He could be on acid, the way he holds them
to the light and stares. "Wow,
man. Heavy. Oh wow . . ."
The way the fingers move—in a group,
or one by one. The way they bend
and straighten out. The way the thumb
is like the others, but different.
The nails. The joints.
The wrinkled palms.

How do these pertain to me?
he thinks in some pre-verbal way.
He wants something to happen.
Poof!—it does.
                    I'm witnessing
the birth of Magic. I'm watching
the genesis of God: *What makes it
happen? Some Power does!*

Erik's mouth gapes, and he squeals
as I lift him high. "Wavy
gravy! Far out, man,"
say his eyes. They grow
wide with ecstasy
when I hand him a seahorse toy,
and it starts to whine,
"It's A Small World"—
not, for once, a cutesy piece
of Disney exploitation,
but a melody pure and Orphean:
the world's first song.

LIBRARIAN'S SON

Mom smiled to see me open
the thick door of a hardcover,
greet the green bookworm that said,
"This book belongs to Charlie Webb,"
and spend a rainy day with Penrod,
Long John, Huckleberry Finn.

She didn't smile to see me reading
*Superman, Fantastic Four, Wonder
Woman* (in star-spangled tights),
Sheena (the tan-legged Jungle Queen).
They were unwelcome as Dewayne,
who I snuck to see—whose tattooed

father swore, and reeked of beer—
who lived in a shack with rusting cars
and chickens in the back. Dewayne,
who loaned me *Leatherneck Tales,*
Monsters Unchained, The Lurking Fear.
I buried them like vampires

under Candyland and Uncle Wiggly,
but they rattled my toy chest
to get out. "Let's go," they hissed,
pulling me away from sunny
playgrounds with mowed grass
into swamps that breathed malaria

and sulfur mist. Rabid wolves
bared bloody fangs there. Fetid
flowers dizzied me (though less
than Yankee Pasha's slave girls).
Melville's bare-breasted Marquesans
wiggled on my lap as Mike Hammer

offered me his smoking "gat,"
warm whiskey, dark ale steeped
in bitters, wine I guzzled
to the dregs, and cigarettes I sucked
till I threw up, then staggered
from the bookmobile, burning for more.

HEAT WAVE

It's all we speak of, like protesters chanting
"Hot, hot, hot!" We feel the scorching sides
of buildings, and kneel to touch the griddle-street.

Rose petals sear in the sun's flame.
Women go bra-less; men wear tee-shirts
to the office; everybody understands.

You can get heat stroke just watching the Hassidim
in beards, black wool suits, fur hats.
Old people broil in their apartments,

heat's hand covering their mouths—
not enough hearses to hold them, not enough
refrigerators to contain the reek.

A 300-pound man chases a 95-pound woman
off a bridge when she sideswipes his Cadillac.
His lawyer claims she jumped "to beat the heat."

The city hums with cicadas and "A.C."s.
I'd have killed for air conditioning in the days
we poor kids packed the public pools,

dog-paddling, cannon-balling as the sun
shrivelled our weed-filled parks and lawns.
We prayed to gods of Watermelon and Pepsi,

slept with wet towels on our feet, and woke
swimming in sweat, as I just did,
boiled out of dreams where—tanned, shirtless—

I rounded third and dug for home
on a sweltering summer day from which the fire
has long died out, but not the heat.

KING SOLOMON'S HIT MAN
—for Zackie

When Solomon needed someone whacked—General Joab,
or his own brother Adonijah—Benaiah was there.

He was in the Bible, so I prayed: "Benaiah, son
of Jehoiada, make Kenny Walters not pinch me."

I burned a black candle to raise Benaiah's ghost.
If he possessed me, Mrs. Sims, who told homeroom,

"Zack sometimes cries crocodile tears," would've leapt
down a croc's gullet before she'd mess with me.

I pictured "Ben" as the museum's ten-foot-tall Assyrian
gate-guard: squared-bearded, pitiless as stone.

He *slew a lion in a pit on a snowy day;* so he was strong,
not claustrophobic or afraid of catching cold.

He *smote two ariels of Moab* (impressive but mysterious).
He skewered a giant on the guy's own giant spear.

As victims *wallowed in their blood,* did big Ben think
"So end all traitors!" Even, "Man, I love this job"?

Or did he feel like I did when that drifter (the cops
called him) jumped me and Kimmi in the woods:

gut-purging fear as his knife slashed my arm
and Kimmi screamed—red, scalding pain as I swung

the ax I'd brought to cut a Christmas tree,
then cold fury as the blade dug in and I kept swinging,

then just cold, like when you're lost in snow, starting
to freeze, and you know it, and you don't care.

POST-MODERN LIFE

> Everything happens "ironically . . . as if between invisible
> quotation marks."
> > —David Lehman, "The Questions of Postmodernism"

The more I swear "I'm serious," the louder guffaws grow.
"Have a nice day" scalds my ears with irony. "Sorry
to hear that," prances by in spike heels and a fake mustache.
"This is great sausage," I attest, and great sausages of the past
rise like ectoplasmic blimps above the table: Sausage Ideals
before which my pale offering festers and stinks
while my guests think, "Ridiculous to praise dead meat!"

All words in black-tie must wear quotation marks, too:
I "regret" to tell you, it's "malignant."
The "wedding" will "unfortunately" not "occur."
The "baby" has "spina bifada" and will be "profoundly retarded."
How "dare" you "address" my "wife" as "Hamster-hips?"
"Hell," your "wife" never "loved" "you";
I've been "sleeping with" "old Hamster hips" for "years."

You "flocking bustard," I'm going to "kick"
the "living horsehair" out of "you"—the boot-to-my-groin,
if your threat proves true, ironic reference
to the time when there were real cowboys
who herded real cows on genuine range,
who wore plain boots (not glittering with ostrich skin
and camp) to keep authentic rattlesnakes from biting,

and to fit in actual stirrups, helping the cowboy stay
on his sure'nough horse, and not be bucked off,
hit his head on bona fide rock, and do what people nowadays—
for instance, you—even with tubes in all your cavities,
machines breathing for you, every organ
in your body failing—must do with a knowing "wink,"
an ironic "cough of blood," a last bored "sigh."

ENGLISH

For years, it meant identifying *noun, verb, adjective,*
or napping as Miss Dewlap droned "Evangeline."

       The Beatles' English meant Carnaby Street:
       birds in *bellbottoms;* pounding *Mersey* rock.

Still, though I came from *English stock,*
the language seemed alien, like smoke I sucked

       into my lungs and blew back out. I never guessed
       that, without English, the *doobies* I puffed,

the *wine coolers* that sluiced down my chin
on sticky August nights, would disappear.

       The *nights* would too, sucked into the unconscious *void.*
       Even that void would vanish, unable to maintain

the non-substance of its nothingness. A pencil might
still half-exist as a *lapiz. Le ciel* might keep

       a shadowy trace of *bleu.* But there would be no more
       abominations. No *breasts, soul kisses,* or *Mr. Stiffie.*

No one could be truculent, *glum, dyspeptic,*
concupiscent, stoked, inscrutable.

       Who'd practice *loan sharking* without *vigorish?*
       The girl I dragged out of Green Lake would have drowned

without the *crawl stroke* and *resuscitate.*
Losing English, I'd be empty as the man who woke

       from a coma, IQ intact, but unable to love.
       No wonder *televangelists* adore The *Word!*

God molded me with English out of formlessness,
and blew between my lips the tongue that made Him.

Praising English, I use it every day,
and pray the *world* that I create with it is *good*.

TAMING MY EXCESSES

"It may be that his verbal talent needs containment
of some kind to tame its natural excesses."
                                    —from a review

A single spotlight hits my sequined suit,
showering sparks into the crowd under
the billowing red-and-gold silk tent.
Bass viols grunt the *Jaws* theme.
Tympanists thunder. My rings—
sapphire, diamond, emerald, ruby,
Tanzanite: one for each finger, plus a
robin-egg-sized pearl on my thumb—
spit fireworks as the cage door clangs
like Doom's guillotine falling. Hey, it's
hard not to feel doomed, alone in my
hoop of light, only de Sade's favorite
whip and Louis Quinze's most rococo
chair between me, The Great Talento,
and my excesses, rumbling and reeking
in the dark. Haven't I worked years to
train them—speaking softly, offering
bits of prime rib which they slap away,
then chomp my hand? Haven't I sent
them to juvie hall, county jail, state
penitentiary, yet they still mock
authority and won't learn a trade?
Haven't coaches, drill instructors, shave-
headed guards made them sprint till
they collapsed, flogged them bloody,
hung them by their heels and sprayed
cold water in their faces, left them in
"The Hole" with rats and lice for com-
pany, yet they've emerged less repentant
than before? Haven't I dressed them in
uniforms and bussed them to Catholic
school, where they blew stink bombs
in confession, chugalugged communion

wine, hailed Mary in tongues so
diabolical three exorcists turned into
macaques and fled screeching? Haven't
I sent them for years to Twelve Step
Programs, yet they stay moral
paralytics? Haven't I fed them truck-
loads of Valium, plus enough
neuroleptics to teach all China the
Thorazine Shuffle? Haven't chemical
castration and gene therapy failed them
utterly? Haven't I jammed them into
sonnets, villanelles, sestinas, sapphics,
rondelles, pantoums, skeltonics, and
clerihews, from every one of which
they burst like Rodan from earth's
flaming core? I hope, then, I may be
forgiven if my chair trembles, and my
whip falls limp when every house-light
suddenly slams on, the crowd gasps,
and my excesses—"part basilisk, part
Blob, part Medusa-haired criminal
defense lawyer, part Hydra-headed
Congressman, each head the size, and
exhaling the atmosphere of Jupiter,"
the papers say—when these excesses
appear to each spectator as his or her
larger, better-looking twin, who
grabbed the best of everything, danced
flamenco on the Golden Mean, hogged
all the fun, yet has the gall to grin and
nod hello, and then—as if out for a
morning constitutional—strides from
the cage into the crowd who, feeling
themselves shrivel more and more, tear down the tent and trample each
other in an undisciplined stampede out the door.

CAR STARTING LATE AT NIGHT

The sound slams its invisible brick
through our front window. Has a burglar
found my emergency cash, and carted off
the new TV? Is some lucky dog
leaving his lover's bed to grab a few winks
before work? Or is he racing home,
thinking of his wife, "She's gonna kill me"?

Has some sloven's mother finally kicked him out?
Maybe the driver is a woman, the last straw
stabbed between her shoulder blades.
Or some granddad who couldn't sleep for dreams
of trout, has—high on coffee—hit the road.
Could enemies have tracked me here?
Any second, the bomb they left may blow;

the fire they started, thrust up its devil-tines.
It could be noon outside. I could have overslept
and missed my meeting, plane, exam.
My wife could have been replaced
by an evil twin, while I fade like a photo
undeveloping, going a black which could
be death, or just the sleep I can't hold back.

I should get up, test every lock, check on my son.
But one by one, my fears drop down
like shooting-gallery banditos. The carnie-man
hands me a teddy bear. Its fur smooths
shut my eyes. There's a little cave inside:
a safe place to sleep all winter, just enough
room for one little family.

III

when, in the first movement of the Emperor Concerto,
where Beethoven tries to out-swagger Napoleon,
a woodpecker countered with Bronx cheers.
Next, every sprinkler on the grassy
amphitheater squeaked on, and listeners fled
as if the Little General's cavalry
had thundered, sabers flashing, from the woods.

The Rondo took a whupping, too,
when a squirrel in the oak that spread
above the stage, banged acorns off the soloist's head
and his ebony Grand. The setting sun
scorched through dark columns of trees
behind the stage as the new soloist marched on.
Her blonde hair glowed, angelic as the tones

she drew, just tuning, from her violin.
We strained forward as her hands caressed
the wood. She was deep into
Tchaikovsky's canzonetta, where he mourns
his unconsummated marriage, when a woman's voice
rose from behind the trees: "Oh God,"
it trilled, a clear coloratura. "Oh, oh, oh!"

What could the soloist do but keep playing?
What could the conductor do but wag
his baton? What could the damp audience do
but shush our children, pretending
not to hear the woman's sobbing obbligato
merge into the theme? And when the finale
began, allegro vivacissimo, and the soloist

lashed her instrument into a gallop,
it seemed natural that the woman's cries
should intensify, and the soloist draw strength
from her as together they approached
that last exhausting run up the scale of passion
toward the summit from which, gasping
and quivering, they flung themselves.

When the paroxysm was done, and the conductor
dropped his hands, and the violinist (on whose
slim legs, seen through her violet gown, I could
have played a pretty tune) lowered her bow,
the applause that surged up out of the soaked grass
was for the woman in the woods as much
as for the soloist: head bowed, smiling. Spent.

BAT BOY JOINS UP
  —*Weekly World News*

In a photo leaked by the Pentagon, the little mutant
wears bandoleers crossed over khaki. A Marine helmet
shoves down his pointed ears. Eight years after being found
in a West Virginia cave, Bat Boy's English is garbled,
but his desire's clear: sink fangs into his country's enemies!

His great strength, his keen sense of smell and hearing,
his ability to scale rock walls and navigate in darkness
make him ideal to hunt people in caves. True, his use
violates international law. But what's too cruel
for fiends who used a country's openness to murder

thousands, and want to germ / gas / nuke the rest?!
On the other hand, these "fiends" claim self defense.
Given slavery and the Indians, don't their fears make sense?
Thoughtful people have to ask: artists, intellectuals, the flowers
of civilization. (Or are we pinworms, sucking anal blood?)

Is patriotism obsolete? Scorning it helped me worm
out of Vietnam. (Is war ever a smart choice for a grunt?)
I'd never follow Bat Boy and enlist, though I may
tell the CIA my plan to flood the Muslim world with Korans
saying Allah made women to govern men. Yesterday,

my wife's hair-dryer fried every circuit in our house.
Turns out the house was wired with lamp-cord.
Char-marks in the attic showed where three fires had been.
While I sweated anthrax and hijacked jet planes,
my family could have charbroiled in our sleep!

Please, God, send Bat Boy to the previous owners.
Let them wake feeling his teeth . . . But wait—
is that Christian? Humane? My dad despised
life insurance; so do I. Is it genetic? If a trait's biochemical,
is it my fault? Does fault exist? Can cheapskates

be otherwise? Can terrorists? Can the U.S.?
Are Indians to blame if fire-water makes them crazed?
Some modern ones harpooned a gray whale,
called devil-fish for attacking schooners twice their size.
Sure enough, the whale rammed the Indians' boat. *Hooray*

for the gray, thought I, who burned, at 10, to be a whaler
(bare Polynesian boombas were involved). It seemed only fair
that the harpooneer's spare skewered his own thigh;
but I stopped reading when his friends emptied assault rifles
into the whale's head. There's fealty to the old ways!

They might as well have sicced Bat Boy on the poor beast.
Would he kill the gophers in my yard?
I nursed a bougainvillea through a withering summer;
now, when it's pink-ruffled as a Mexican dancer,
gophers are going for its roots. My family's first week here

(as the attic charred), our cat left five dead gophers
on the porch. Now suddenly the cat is old.
All day she loafs on my lawn chair. As punishment,
I squirt her with the hose. Is that mature? Or kind?
Is it worth trying to be what I clearly am not?

If Bat Boy wants to rip out terrorists' throats, isn't that good?
If he kills civilians too, is that our problem?
When my friend's son asked to be a vampire for Halloween,
his mom bought him a pumpkin suit: non-violent, non-scary,
non-fun. No one makes Bat Boy costumes,

but I'll bet someone makes Arab terrorists. Some kid
will wear one, and get shot. Some innocent pumpkin
will eat an anthrax-dusted Tootsie Roll. Think that's far-fetched?
The governor publicized "credible threats" to bomb
the Golden Gate Bridge at rush hour. Muslims (I hear)

buy gas stations to blow them up, 7-Elevens to poison
the Big Gulps, and motels to burn travelers in their sleep.
Anything's likely with the Twin Towers down—
though, by the way, I don't believe there's a Bat Boy, or God,
or one right way to look at things.

                           I wish there was.

A MEAL NOT EATEN

"Somewhere there's an uneaten Chinese dinner with our
name on it."

—Overheard

The wonton soup drifts in warm fog
just out of reach. Dragons circle
the bowl as if to guard the one
pink shrimp that bobs like a dead
monster-from-the-deep. Steam

wisps off the twice-cooked
pork and chopped bok choy.
The Emperor's Chicken is here too:
sliced peppers, red and green;
black mushroom-gongs; white

meat glistening in glaze. We feed
each other between kisses, screened
by our red leather booth, ignoring
vines that loop and dangle
overhead, the waiters gliding

back and forth, so unobtrusive
it's as if platters fly solo through the air.
One floats toward us, bearing
orange-halves offered
in their bowls of pebbled skin.

Fortune cookies' brittle purses enfold
futures that, like this past,
never occurred. I didn't pay
the bill, open her door, or drive her
to my house, where we never

made love in this bed where I lie now,
in which I can almost touch her,
asleep beside me as my wife,
though she is not, and hasn't been
for a long time.

BRAIN DAMAGE

Kittens scamper within weeks. Baby
turtles crack their eggs and stroll away.
But it takes months for a human to roll over,
a year to walk—all so the brain can grow big

enough to sustain a conversation,
multiply fractions, and once in a long while,
paint Mona Lisa, or entertain $E=mc2$.
The slightest damage could prevent that,

I think, pinching *tsunomono*
between chopsticks at Aoba Restaurant.
Just as I'm savoring the vinegary crunch,
Erik lunges for Kate's hot *miso* soup.

"Help me," she yelps. I yank him back.
His head whacks the wooden booth
with a bonk that rocks the place.
"What's wrong with you?" hisses Kate.

Erik shrieks, but in fifty-five seconds,
subsides. We drive home, safe.
I place him in his crib; then, arm
around Kate, watch on TV the story

of a Chinese vase, lost at sea,
but so well-packed that it was found
after three centuries, in pristine condition,
"snug as a brain in its case," the diver says.

MYSTERIES

To lie in this exact bed in this very room,
rain plinking my roof's cedar keys.

To scan the room—think "closet," "heater,"
"dirty sock," and tell the difference.

To watch sunrise silver one strip of my rug,
the rest left pre-Genesis black.

To picture the terrarium where gopher
tortoises rattle their cracked food-plate

and, for all I know, create the world
my jelly-eyes perceive. To lift

my hand and obliterate my bookcase,
which is an enchanted tree.

To feel the warmth inside my bed,
as if my comforter is a blue sun. To see

my shirt on a doorknob, empty of me.
To sense, under cover of skin, the body

I call *mine* pulsing, bubbling,
its battery good for just so many beats—

the sum total of fish I'll catch, and breasts
I'll kiss ticking away—even my thoughts

growing turgid as blood in a clogged vein
until one day I gasp, amazed.

LANDSCAPES
        —For K

To paint them seems redundant in this century.
        "What a lake!" the artist thinks,
                and from his brush-spigot a piddling lake flows.

There's still the pleasure, though, of honing skills:
        painting a field of fireweed
                so that it looks just like a field of fireweed.

There's still the impulse to image what I love
        and see it when I please—and the wish
                to tag the world's wall: "I was here!"

There's emotional expression: picturing the brown
        badlands where my heart's river twists
                beneath maroon storm clouds and lightning-

blasted pines. There's the thrill of fantasy:
        fern-filled Jurassic valley, tarnished slough,
                mountains repeating M into infinity.

A few viewers can almost smell my skunk cabbage,
        almost hear, above the brook trout's slurp,
                my redwings *Kong-ka-reeee!* The rest flock straight

to Modernism as it tugs their legs, raises black impasto
        brows above a corn field, or squats behind red
                toothpaste-glops, shrilling, "Look! Come see!!"

What's it to me? I can still catch, in fading light, the sheen
        of this full moon on onyx water.
                I can state in pigment, "That's the way it was,"

and frame the evidence for hanging where my guests
        can't miss it as they rush in from the snow,
                backs to a view that tacked an extra fifty K to my escrow:

shrubbery mustaches poking through white drifts;
      ducks in a buckshot pattern aimed for violet cliffs
           which overlook the sea, which merges with the place

where dead artists at their easels try to re-create
      the colors we paint just by living underneath
           the clouds' smeared signatures, the blue haze of the sky.

A GRAND OPENING OF HEARTS

Kate and I play Mozart for Erik, read him
Mother Goose, show him "Starry Night,"
wheel his stroller through Descanso Gardens,
pointing out ducks, squirrels, koi,

a basking terrapin, as well as trees, roses,
grass, a lily-pond, the sky's vast blue mobile
hung with clouds "like your stuffed animals."
He flails his limbs, and squalls.

Baffled by this grub, this homunculus
who caricatures me, I pitch my voice as close
as possible to his (its timbre gouged
into my brain), and voice my frustration: "Aaah!"

He looks surprised, then replies, "Aaah!"
I repeat "Aaah!" He says it back.
His hands punch with excitement.
I assert, "Aaah!" "Aaah!" he agrees.

It's not Plato & Socrates,
but it *is* flight across a sea-sized
chasm of consciousness. It is
a confluence of minds, and a Grand

Opening of hearts. And it gives rise
to another first for him (but not a last
if I have any "Aaah" in the matter):
an upward curving of the lips

that evokes the same from me,
as when two friends, long-separated,
waiting for take-out in a strange city,
happen to look up, and their eyes meet.

AMATEURS

A backyard astronomer charts two new supernovas
in one night. A janitor at MIT solves in an hour
a math problem that's stumped the faculty for years.
So what if that was in a movie? It could happen.
Gregor Mendel was a monk; John Priestly, a minister.

Charles Darwin studied medicine *and* ministry
before he clumped aboard The Beagle. Einstein
was a patent clerk. And how about sports?
Forget the agents fluffing athletes like prize poodles.
Forget mega-contracts with incentives actually

to play. While product endorsements are thin
clouds on the horizon, watch (between commercials)
virgins who've barely been tongue-kissed by fame
perform Olympian feats for fun, excitement, love.
Consider us: uninstructed in tantric sex, innocent

of psychotherapy. How fearlessly you explore
my steppes, jungles, valleys, and peaks.
Night after night, I chart the galaxies inside your eyes.
You discover the mechanics of my breath,
the calculus of my heart accelerated by your kiss.

Daily we find new tonics and miracle cures.
We break thermodynamics's laws, out-muscle
biochemistry's tightest bonds. We speedboat off
the edge of the known world, and it extends beneath us
even while, as lovers always have, we fly.

HUMMINGBIRDS

Who, in cold lands where hummingbirds
    are rare, would see a bee-like bird,
and not a wee green man or pixie girl

    in emerald gown, with crystal wings?
Who wouldn't hear in hummingbirds'
    metallic twitters, elfin tongues?

Finding a nest the size of a child's teacup,
    woven of moss, lichens, spider web,
who wouldn't think some fairy princess

    had slept there, naming her Titania,
Tinkerbell, or Calothorax *lucifer* (light-bearing,
    as the morning star)? Who, seeing a creature

sip from lily-throats, emerging covered
    with gold pollen, wouldn't think of fairy dust?
Who wouldn't see sequin-sized feathers—

    ruby, pink, azure, magenta—as coats
of iridescent mail, and feel the wearers
    of such wealth could call down mist, and weave

rainbows—that they could turn invisible
    (buzzing off, too quick to see)—that they came
from a world untouched by disease or time,

    where a mortal who spent one day,
then returned to his own land, would find
    his friends long dead, himself an old, old man?

DOES TIME REALLY EXIST?

It seems to, when I'm late for work. Clocks
argue for it ardently. People's absence—
Mom, Dad, Isaac Newton, Bela Lugosi—
suggests the vampire Time has had its way. Yet

physicist Julian Barbour calls time "illusory."
An equation that describes the shape of every
possible universe, and the position of everything
in each (even the reading glasses I misplaced

last night?) is best solved by eliminating time.
Each instant may be a different universe,
like frames in a movie—say, *The Time Machine*,
which Rod Taylor may still be filming somewhere.

If that's true, I've never stopped wolfing Mom's
pot roast while the Christmas tree shimmers
by my new cherry-red bike. Romeo's and Juliet's
nemesis, Dawn, still hasn't touched Linda and me,

my family visiting in Baltimore while I stay home
for summer school. Of course, I have mumps forever,
and have to hear Carol Kamas explain, in perpetuity,
how much she loves her ex-boyfriend, who's back . . .

These days, I try to squeeze all the pleasure I can
from things like shoving a shopping cart
through Safeway with no lumbar pain, and only slight
congestion in my head. Before I leave for work,

I peel an orange, and make myself savor every slice.
Even if time exists, I can freeze-frame by writing,
Sweet orange pulp sticks between my teeth.
Orange-juice rivers slither down my tongue.

SEDUCING SLEEP

Lie back and let her make the moves.
Don't chase her with your arms outstretched,
screaming, "I need!" To those insomniacs

who jab microphones into her face—
"Why go into exile? When will you
return?"—she barks, "No comment,"

as her limo leaves them, wide-eyed,
in the dust. Night's squirmers, flailers,
cover-twirlers pray to Sleep. They burn

incense, play soothing music, offer presents
of cookies and milk, but never catch
their goddess's nose, or ear, or eye.

A Christmas tricycle or morning biopsy
will drive Sleep from the snuggest bed.
Pills and potions may summon a dark tide

that feels like Sleep; but instead of leaving
fertile soil for the new day, they salt
the earth, or scour it down to bare rock.

How different when, after rattling
six hours in my truck, I lurch and crunch
down the gravel road to Lenice Lake.

As coyotes yip, and dawn's first purple
dims the stars, I launch my boat
on black water boiling with trout

that I hook, whooping, as the sun's
gold heater soars. Then Sleep,
whom I've tantalized for hours, wraps

soft hands around my eyes. I lie back—
hat over my face as the lake rocks me—
and let her have her way.

SCUBA HEAVEN

Too much air in your vest,
and you bob like an apple.
Too little air, you sink

faster and faster as the water's
hand—larger and larger—
shoves you down.

Pump in just enough air,
though, and you fall slowly,
as in dreams. Coral lifts

purple arms to you. Fish
fly up like welcoming putti.
The weight of aging falls

away. Cares that compress
your spine on land,
and make you shorter

every day, bubble up
and out, turned cool
and crystalline. You could be

a hawk, floating high
above its canyon home—
a planet, hung suspended

in the sky. You recognize
bat-winged mantas
as seraphim, and God

as a huge ulua in a cave
at ninety feet. Hover;
the Divine will rise to you.

TAKING OUT TRASH

There's more to it than spilling our red garbage can
into the city's big blue bin. I have to slip
from bed without waking my wife. (I pretend

I'm a silk handkerchief, the bed's a pocket;
then I pick myself.) I sneak past my boy's
bedroom, where he lies submerged in sleep.

Easing shut the kitchen door, I stuff yesterday's
news in the *Recycle* bag. I dump
the pork chow mein that Kate brought home

from lunch, and forgot to refrigerate.
After sponging the placemats (apricot-cake crumbs,
dry scraps of beef that Erik missed),

I wash a dish of congealed oatmeal down
the sink, and toss the junk mail
I left out to "think about." (Should I compare

insurance rates? Would anyone I know enjoy
a *Gone with the Wind* porcelain egg?)
I scratch the cat's ears, replenish her liver-

and-shrimp, sift the offerings from her catbox,
and drop them in the Hefty-bag-lined
garbage can. When our gate squeaks,

I think (as usual), "Got to oil that,"
as I consign the Hefty bag to the blue bin.
Back in the house, I close the door quietly,

turn on the furnace, and by its proxy,
nudge my family awake with a warm hand—
I, who used to wear my guitar like a chasuble,

invoking God through a Shure microphone.
I: a former stand-in for Zeppelin and The Stones,
who thought he was a most important man.

HOW TO LIVE

> *"I don't know how to live."*
> —*Sharon Olds*

Eat lots of steak and salmon and Thai curry and mu shu
pork and fresh green beans and baked potatoes
and fresh strawberries with vanilla ice cream.
Kick-box three days a week. Stay strong and lean.
Go fly-fishing every chance you get, with friends

who'll teach you secrets of the stream. Play guitar
in a rock band. Read Dostoyevsky, Whitman, Kafka,
Shakespeare, Twain. Collect Uncle Scrooge comics.
See Peckinpah's *Straw Dogs*, and everything Monty Python made.
Love freely. Treat ex-partners as kindly

as you can. Wish them as well as you're able.
Snorkel with moray eels and yellow tangs. Watch
spinner dolphins earn their name as your *panga* slam-
bams over glittering seas. Try not to lie; it sours
the soul. But being a patsy sours it too. If you cause

a car wreck, and aren't hurt, but someone is, apologize
silently. Learn from your mistake. Walk gratefully
away. Let your insurance handle it. Never drive drunk.
Don't be a drunk, or any kind of "aholic." It's bad
English, and bad news. Don't berate yourself. If you lose

a game or prize you've earned, remember the winners
history forgets. Remember them if you *do* win. Enjoy
success. Have kids if you want and can afford them,
but don't make them your reason-to-be. Spare them that
misery. Take them to the beach. Mail order sea

monkeys once in your life. Give someone the full-on
ass-kicking he (or she) has earned. Keep a box turtle
in good health for twenty years. If you get sick, don't thrive
on suffering. There's nothing noble about pain. Die
if you need to, the best way you can. (You define *best*.)

Go to church if it helps you. Grow tomatoes to put *store-
bought* in perspective. Listen to Elvis and Bach. Unless
you're tone deaf, own Perlman's "Meditation from Thais."
Don't look for hidden meanings in a cardinal's song.
Don't think TV characters talk to you; that's crazy.

Don't be too sane. Work hard. Loaf easily. Have good
friends, and be good to them. Be immoderate
in moderation. Spend little time anesthetized. Dive
the Great Barrier Reef. Don't touch the coral. Watch
for sea snakes. Smile for the camera. Don't say "Cheese."

THE END

Usually, we're warned. The author dons
an elegiac tone. The voice begins
to roll—deepening the way a pastor's drone

draws resonance from a grave open
at his feet. Like the last hours of summer
vacation, the story's running out.

No wonder my throat tightens, and the letters
blur. It's Time I hear pronouncing Fin—
not Time the Sneak, dropping a new

transparency on me daily, changing me
so slowly I forget what's happening,
but Time the Bully, jeering "Aw, get old

and die!" As the conclusion rushes at me
like the ground during a fall, I picture Mom
waving the day I left for college. I feel

Linda's arms the night she moved
with her family to Maine. I see myself
scrounging for one last sand-dollar—

burgers eaten, ice chest dumped, waves
starting to phosphoresce as Dad fires up
the blue Buick and Mom calls, "Honey, time to go."

I remember Dad's first *transient global
amnesia*, that cleared in hours, but left
black buzzards circling his brain. I mourn

the sun squeezing behind the one tree
in this parking lot as I close my book
to save the last page for later, and waitresses

in khaki shorts bounce to their shifts
at the Elephant Bar: eight hours they think
will drag on endlessly.

IN THE BEGINNING WAS THE WORD

Scientists agree that it was "BANG,"
roared in a voice so big it blew the universe
out of a hole tinier than the smallest germ.

No wonder Erik—twenty-pound image
of God—is so well pleased with his first word:
"Cat," blurted one day in our back yard

when Kiki, our Abyssinian, charged by,
chasing a maple leaf. No wonder
Erik thought he'd called her into being,

and when he sees her now, explodes "CAT,"
proud as if he's created a world.
No wonder he learns new words—

cool, yuck, car, play—since the first
packed so much punch, his mom and me
applauding like angels at the Big Guy's feet.

No wonder Erik runs into the living room,
shouting "SOCK," and holding one.
No wonder he sees me put on shoes,

points, bellows "SHOE," laughs with glee,
and runs in circles, power-wild.
No wonder I forget his dripping diapers,

as well as the fishing trips, scuba dives,
and sexy nights his life denies my wife and me
when, as I heat his oatmeal in the kitchen,

he screams "DA-DA," then bear-hugs
the leg of this adult he's made. No wonder
I'm proud that, one November night

my wife and I, at the right moment,
both exclaimed with our whole bodies,
"BOY!"